Special Tagine

Moroccan Tagine

Best Moroccan Tagine recipes

By The Elite Moroccan Chef

- This book is presented to you by indigenous Moroccans who are fond of cooking and have experience with original Moroccan cooking.

History of Moroccan cuisine:

Moroccan cuisine is known for mixing it with several kitchens such as Arab, Middle Eastern, Mediterranean, African, and Maghreb kitchens And Berber. Moroccan cuisine is the second in the world after French, and it is the first in the African and Arabic world.

Features of Moroccan food:

It is characterized by its wide use of vegetables and fruits, as well as meat, poultry and fish. Spices and condiments are among the ingredients main Moroccan meals, such as saffron, ginger, black and red pepper, and others.

Among the most famous Moroccan dishes:

- Couscous
- Bastilla
- Mrouzia
- Tangia
- Al-Zaalouk
- The Harsha
- Al-Baghrir
- Rfaisa
- Al Harira
- Malwi

Among the most famous Moroccan sweets:

- Cakes with honey

- Chebakia

- Coke desserts

- Kaab Ghazal

Contents

Special Tagines :

Moroccan tagines are one of the most delicious foods that you have to try in order to enjoy a hearty and delicious meal. Moroccan tagines recipes are considered the master of family occasions, because they carry a variety of food ingredients to suit all tastes, and lovers of strong meals that combine meat, chicken and vegetables, made with the secret recipe that bears the imprint of Moroccan cuisine, the recipes of tajine have become roaming the world, due to the popularity they find, in addition to the desire of visitors to eat and the desire to taste the most delicious Moroccan tagine recipes.

The most delicious Moroccan tagines and their   action steps:

Moroccan chicken recipe :

One of the most delicious Moroccan tagines is the delicious chicken recipe that must be prepared to experience the authentic Moroccan taste.

The ingredients :

- Two medium-sized onions, chopped

- 8 cloves of peeled garlic

- A cup of chickpeas

- Two tablespoons of ghee

- 20 cardamom pods

- 3 sticks of cinnamon

- 4 cloves

- 9 grains of anise flower

- A teaspoon of black pepper

- Teaspoon salt

- 10 chicken thighs

- 3 cups of water

- 1/4 kilo black olives without seeds

- 6 pickled lemons

- A cup of soaked raisins

- Two tablespoons of white sugar

- A teaspoon of saffron

- From 15 to 20 dried apricots

- Pinch of paprika

- A few pistachios and almonds

Marinade For Chicken :

- 1 tablespoon of cinnamon

- 1 tablespoon of turmeric

- 2 tablespoons of salt

- 1 tablespoon ground ginger

- 1 tablespoon of cumin

- 4 tablespoons of flour

- 1 tablespoon of dried coriander

- 1 tablespoon of paprika

How to prepare chicken Tagine:

1. In a Tefal frying pan over medium heat, put the onion rings and oil, then add the spices and garlic to it, turn them over and simmer for a few minutes.

2. Leave the chicken thighs well in their marinade, then add to the pan with onions and stir together. Leave for half an hour on the fire with light stirring, and then add the water and the chickpeas.

3. Put the dry chicken spices in the clay casserole, add onions, lemon slices, and chicken thighs, close the tajine with aluminum foil tightly, then enter the oven and leave for an hour or less on hot heat.

4. Then reduce the oven temperature and leave the casserole as it is inside for half an hour.

5. Take out the tagine and add to it the dried apricots, soaked raisins, paprika, and a pinch of black pepper and leave for the third time in the oven for ten minutes, after which we completely remove the aluminum foil cover and leave the tagine a little brown.

6. The tagine is served as is, with the addition of pistachios and almonds on the top for decoration, a simple workshop of paprika and olives scattered.

Moroccan Tagine meat with Dates:

Meat with dates is one of the traditional tajines of the Moroccan people, which is considered one of the most welcoming dishes that the people are interested in preparing banquets.

The ingredients:

- 3 tablespoons of olive oil
- 750 grams of lamb, cut into cubes
- 250 grams of dates without pits
- Two large onions, chopped
- Two tablespoons of fresh tomato sauce
- 4 cloves of minced garlic
- One tablespoon of ginger
- 3 tablespoons of roasted pine nuts
- One tablespoon of cinnamon
- Pinch of saffron
- two big spoons of lemon juice
- 1 tablespoon of spices
- 1 tablespoon of grated lemon peel
- Two cubes of meat broth
- Two tablespoons of honey

• Half a kilo of ready-made couscous

How to prepare meat tagine with dates:

1. In a large deep frying pan containing a spoonful of oil, place it on medium heat and fry the meat cubes on all sides, until it changes color.

2. Then remove the meat cubes from the pan and put them in the casserole, and leave it aside.

3. Add the rest of the oil to the same pan, and after that the chopped onions, and stir over the fire until wilted, then add the garlic and spices (salt, chili, black pepper), ginger, saffron, and cinnamon.

4. Turn them all over with the onions, then crumble the meat broth on top of them, then put the mixture on the casserole over the meat cubes, and cover the tagine with tin foil.

5. Heat the oven to a temperature of 250 degrees, then put the casserole inside and leave it for 90 minutes. After that, take out the casserole dish and add the tomato sauce/honey, all the dates, grated lemon, and juice, and return to the oven for 25 minutes.

6. The tagine is ready to be served after putting the finishing touches, which is to pour the tagine over the couscous and decorate it in a circular motion with roasted pine nuts.

Moroccan Chicken Tagine with vegetables:

One of the healthy Tagines, full of varieties of vegetables that are prepared in the Moroccan way.

The ingredients:

- 3 large onions, medium size
- 3 tablespoons of chopped parsley
- A whole chicken
- 4 tablespoons of olive oil
- 3 tablespoons of chopped green coriander
- 4 large tomatoes, chopped
- 3 zucchini, chopped
- Two carrots cut into cubes
- 5 medium-sized potatoes, cut into cubes
- One tablespoon of powdered ginger
- 1/2 teaspoon of saffron leaves
- 3 sticks of cinnamon
- 5 cups of water
- 2 cubes of chicken stock
- A cup of fresh green olives

How to prepare the Tagine:

1. Fry the onions in a large bowl over low heat, until they turn golden in color, then add the olives to them, and continue stirring.

2. Cut the chicken into medium-sized pieces, wash it well with water, salt and lemon, then season with black pepper and salt, and leave it for two hours.

3. Put the chicken in the bowl, add the water, broth, ginger, and cinnamon, then stir them together, then add saffron and leave them together until the chicken is tender.

4. Then add all the vegetables and saute with the chicken, and leave until the chicken is tender too.

5. Then place the chicken on a serving plate and garnish with parsley and coriander

The most delicious Moroccan tagines, steamed meat:

One of the best Moroccan recipes is the popular Moroccan steamed meat recipe.

The ingredients:

- 3 kilos of lamb chops large size (bones are kept)

- 1/2 kilo of green beans

- 4 carrots

- Two cauliflower cups

- 4 medium-sized onions

- 4 cloves of minced garlic

- A tablespoon of saffron

- Two cups of animal ghee

- A tablespoon of salt

- 1/2 tablespoon of cumin

- 1/2 tablespoon of black pepper

How to prepare the tagine:

1. Rub the meat pieces with salt, black pepper, and saffron, then place them in a pressure cooker that contains half of water for at least 3 hours.

2. Put a large and deep frying pan on the fire, then put the animal ghee inside and add the ripe meat pieces to it.

3. The meat is stirred in the ghee on a medium ignition heat. After its color changes, it is poured into a large tray, then placed inside the oven until its color turns golden completely.

4. During this, place the vegetables (carrots, onion rings, and bean cloves), chopped garlic, and cumin in a pressure cooker, leave on the fire until cooked, then spread evenly on a serving plate.

5. To decorate the steamed meat in the Moroccan way, be placed on top of it, and saffron and a little cumin are sprinkled on top.

6. The tagine is eaten hot and served with rice or prepared couscous.

Moroccan sardine Tagine :

Moroccan sardine casserole and Morocco has a special charm, especially its atmosphere and beauty, and what distinguishes it most is Moroccan food, especially Moroccan tagines, food cooked with pottery has a special distinctive flavor and gives the food an irresistible taste, today we will present the sardine casserole for fish lovers with chermoula.

The ingredients of the Moroccan sardine Tagine:

- A kilo of sardines
- 2 tomatoes
- 2 green capsicum
- 4 celery sticks
- 2 lemon slices
- Olive oil for spreading the casserole dish
- A cup of coffee water
- One green hot pepper

Charmoula:

- Parsley washed and finely chopped
- Garlic head, crushed
- Lemon juice
- A quarter of a small spoon of red pepper
- A quarter of a teaspoon of black pepper
- Salt, to taste

- A tablespoon of cumin
- A cup of olive oil coffee
- A small spoonful of vinegar spirit
- 1 teaspoon puree
- A small spoon of turmeric

How to prepare:

1- Wash all the vegetables and cut them into thick circular rings, except for   hot green pepper and celery, so sticks remain.

2- Open the sardines in the middle, remove the spines, and wash well.

3- Prepare the strawberry by mixing the ingredients well.

4- Grease the surface of the sardines and the inside of the sardine with a strawberry.

5- Bring the tagine that will be cooked with olive oil.

6- Put 1/2 the amount of sardines in the tagine

7- Then stack the vegetables on top, except for the lemon, then the rest of the amount of sardines, then the lemon, the remainder of the charmoula and hot pepper, add the water and cover.

8- Put in the oven for 45 minutes, until vegetables and fish are cooked.

9 - To be raised and served hot and healthy.

How to make fried eggplant with charmoula sauce:

Here is how to make fried eggplant with charmoula sauce in very easy steps from Moroccan cuisine, which is an easy business recipe for making.

Ingredients for fried eggplant with charmoula sauce:

- 2 eggplant
- 1 teaspoon salt
- 1 clove of crushed garlic
- 1 teaspoon paprika
- Pinch of chili
- ¾ 1 teaspoon cumin
- 3 tablespoons fresh parsley, chopped
- 3 tablespoons chopped fresh coriander
- 3 tablespoons of lemon juice
- ½ cup olive oil

How to make fried eggplant with charmoula sauce:

Cut the eggplant into slices, sprinkle the salt on it, and put it in a colander until it gets rid of the water.

Preheat oven to 180 ° C.

Mix garlic, paprika, cumin, half the amount of parsley, half the amount of coriander, lemon juice.

Mix 2 tablespoons of oil with a pinch of salt and stir.

Drain the eggplant and brush each slice on both sides with olive oil.

Put the eggplant in a tray and put it in the oven for 30 minutes.

Put the rest of the oil in a frying pan and fry the eggplant after leaving the oven until it is slightly crunchy, for a minute on each side.

Put the eggplant in a serving dish and pour the sauce over it and decorate with the rest of the parsley and coriander.

Moroccan Batbout Bread:

And of course, it is advisable to eat the tagine with bread, to pass a better and amazing experience, and among the Moroccan bread there is the Batbout, which is one of the most delicious and wonderful bread.

Moroccan dishes are among the most famous dishes in the Arab Maghreb, and their reputation has reached the Gulf and the world. If you are a fan of Moroccan food and tried Moroccan recipes, we recommend that you familiarize yourself with the recipe for Moroccan duck bread.

To know how easy this bread is, which can be prepared easily and quickly with a regular fryer and the results are impressive and can be kept for a relatively long time in a dry and cool place, and you can reheat when needed, but the pleasure of this bread is that it is prepared fresh for you and your family, especially on holidays, by following the following steps You will get wonderful bread, which is the custom in Morocco, where the housewife prepares bread in the morning for breakfast, and it is also an essential component of the Ramadan table.

The ingredients:

- 1 tablespoon of corn oil
- 1 tablespoon yeast dissolved with a little water and sugar
- 1 teaspoon salt
- 2 cups white flour
- Half a cup of warm water

How to prepare:

Put the flour in a deep bowl and add all of the oil, yeast, salt, then gradually add the water and knead well So that we have a cohesive dough, we cover it and leave it in a warm place until it ferments and is ready for use. We divide the dough into medium-sized balls and let it rest a little, then roll it out with the palm, with a thickness of 1 cm, and let it rest a little after its individual. Heat a non-stick frying pan, and place the dough pieces and turn them over on both sides until they are filled with air and are cooked and our puffed and soft pieces of bread are formed.

Some Moroccan Sweets And How To Prepare Them

Moroccan Ghriba:

A delicious, low-calorie, fast, and easy way to enjoy it with a cup of tea.

The work ingredients of the Moroccan Ghriba:

- Six cups sifted flour
- One and a quarter cup of sugar
- A cup and a half of unsalted butter
- Sesame powder 50 g
- A cup of ground almonds
- Tray condensed milk sweetened
- Three teaspoons and half of ground cinnamon

The way the Moroccan Ghriba works:

1- Mix all the ingredients until it becomes a soft and smooth paste

2- Form small balls and press them slightly with your finger until it becomes a small circle

3- Place the dough circles on a baking tray, making sure to keep a 2-3 cm distance between each grain

4- Bake in the middle of the oven at 170 degrees, until golden

Kaab Al-Ghazal:

Kaab al-Ghazal sweet is one of the most famous Moroccan sweets and is prepared to be served on special occasions. It is somewhat similar to walnut or pistachio, which is a sweet dough stuffed with almonds, and the origin of this dessert dates back 200 years, nearly two centuries, and its name actually goes back to it because it resembles The left foot of the gazelle, which is shaped like a crescent, continues this Moroccan dessert in Fez.

How to prepare Kaab al-Ghazal:

The Egyptian Kaab al-Ghazal differs completely from the Moroccan, but today we offer you the original method of preparing Kaab al-Ghazal according to the original method, and even the Moroccan method prepares it in two different ways and with different ingredients, and we offer you the original method in detail as follows:

Ingredients:

The first way to prepare the Moroccan Kaab Al-Ghazal:

- 2 kilos of peeled almonds.
- A kilo of white sugar.
- A small spoon of mastic.
- A cup of liquid butter.
- A cup of orange blossom water.

Or another amount of ingredients is used to make the Moroccan heel deer, which are:

- A one-quarter kilogram of shelled ground almonds, or the equivalent of 650 grams.
- A carton of approximately 400 grams of sweetened condensed milk.
- A quarter cup of rose water.

Moroccan Kaab Al-Ghazal paste:

Ingredients:

- A kilo of fine white flour for all purposes.
- A cup of orange blossom water.
- Half a spoonful of ground mastic.
- Two cups of liquid butter.
- Pinch of salt.
- Water as needed.

First method:

We prepare the flour and put the ground mastic in the core, butter, and a pinch of salt, and start kneading with the tips of the fingers, then start adding the blossom water and stirring well with the tips of the fingers.

We start by putting in a little hot water so that we can collect the dough.

Put the dough on a dry surface and continue kneading until the dough becomes firm and becomes soft and tender.

We begin to divide the amount into small pieces as desired and start covering the dough and leave it for at least half an hour to rest and facilitate its formation.

We prepare the food processor and put the peeled almonds, the amount of white sugar, the liquid butter at room temperature, the blossom water, and the rose water and mix very well until the filling is homogeneous.

And after it becomes completely smooth, start forming it with little fingers or as desired.

We prepare the dough, take a piece of it and wrap the rest with plastic so that it does not dry out and become damaged.

And we start rolling the dough with mardana or the rolling pin until we get a long and semi-transparent rectangular shape.

We put the finger on the letter of the dough and cover the filling with the dough and begin to thin the filling and the dough in the form of an arched and raised crescent.

We use the round dough cutter to cut the dough.

Get rid of the excess dough, make sure it is airtight, and repeat the steps until all of it runs out.

We prepare the baking tray, brush with butter, and place the pieces in it after forming them.

We begin to make small holes with a clean toothpick and enter the oven at a medium temperature until the face is browned and out of the oven and left until it cools because it is smooth and if it is stirred while it is hot it will break.

It is decorated with peeled almonds and served with hot drinks.

The second method:

Put the almonds and the sweetened condensed milk in the food processor and beat well, and start adding the rose water gradually until the filling holds together well.

We form the filling in the form of fingers of medium size and length.

We begin to prepare an amount of heel dough, the ingredients of which were previously mentioned because the ingredients for the dough are fixed in all methods.

We start shaping it into a thin crescent shape and cut the remainder of the dough with a fluttering circular slicer.

And bring the tray prepared for baking and brush with a measure of liquid butter and enter the oven at a medium temperature, or the equivalent of 180 degrees Celsius, until the face is red and completely cooked.

It is served with delicious drinks, coffee or tea, and for a thousand bliss.

I hope you liked these dishes

By The Elite Moroccan Chef